WILLING TO WORK FORWARD

Published by The Regenerative Writing Institute
www.regenwriting.com

ISBN: 978-1-950779-03-1

GINA TANG

WILLING TO WORK FORWARD

selected poetry & prose

The Regenerative Writing Institute

CONTENTS

CONTENTS

CONTENTS

These words
Are the scattered ashes
Of moments past,
And the wings
Of worlds envisioned.

This book is dedicated to
The courage it takes
To live with an open heart.

Love,
Gina

MEMORY

Phhhft! My Dad spits out the shell of a sunflower seed. The halves fall to the weathered wooden deck. They are shiny with spit. He sits in a white wire chair, wearing only shorts. It's summertime in Seattle, and his smooth skin is warm when I climb onto his lap. He smells like sunlight.

I want a sunflower seed, too. I pop one into my mouth, but I can't crack it open, so I suck on the saltiness instead. I spit it out into my hand when the flavor is gone. My dad looks at the wet, whole shell in my palm. He takes it, puts it up to his teeth, bites down. It cracks open like a black-and-white striped egg, a sunflower egg. *Phhhft!* He spits out the shell, then hands me the seed. I put it into my mouth and chew it. Stale. I like the shell better.

Then I find two pennies, a nickel, and a dime in Dad's pocket. I slide off his lap, onto the deck. I make piles: biggest to smallest, smallest to biggest. There is a dime in my hand when I see the crack between the wooden beams. It is dark and strange through the crack, the mystery that is Under-the-Deck, and it wants to be touched. The dime fits perfectly in the crack. The dime will go where I cannot. I lower the dime. The darkness pulls it, sucks it through, gone. My dad has been watching me. He tells me it is illegal to throw away money.

The sliding door opens, and out comes my sister. She is three but I am five. The blue polka-dot shorts she is wearing used to be mine. I watch her bare feet padding across the deck, hoping she isn't heading for Dad's lap. Instead she sits on the ledge at the edge of the flower beds, looking for big furry bumblebees.

The bees spend a lot of time around a low bushy plant with small pink flowers. They are fat and slow and lazy, hanging in the air like bubbles. I see her finger reaching out. She carefully pets a fuzzy back.

When she smiles, her eyes become crescent moons.

FREEDOM

I asked my friend,
Who had recently died—
What is Freedom?

Here's what he showed me:

Freedom is feeling without borders.
Freedom is faith in disorder.

Freedom is the capacity to compost your shit.
Freedom is failing for the fun of it.

Freedom is permission to be out of your mind.
Freedom is moving to unwind.

Freedom is needing something and saying so.
Freedom is leaving when it's time to go.

Freedom is forgiveness, and abundant grace.
Freedom is knowing that nothing about you
has to change.

Freedom is every flower, rock, and tree.
Freedom is who we came to be.

-For Burt

THE WIND OF CHANGE BLOWS MY MIND

Leaves clap in the breeze
A standing ovation

Wind, air, breath of spirit—
        Moving always
        Moving always

The leaves fall
The petals drop
The towers tumble

Rebirthing
Remothering
Remembering

I am just elasticity
A plasmic plasticity

I am made of this fire, this earth,
this water, this wind

My skin is permeable, perforated—
I am a flute
Instrument in the hand of a master

RISE
and
SHINE

SHELTER

Here, like elsewhere,
We shelter in place—
This heart space,
Our true home.

What rhythms do we hold?

So much of what
We worked for before
Falls away,
Like tears from a face.

As we observe
Ourselves in isolation,
What can we learn?

Presence is required, now,
Not just preferred.

The world is cancelled until further notice.

Tapping into intrinsic wisdom
Without distraction or diversion
(Or with just the right amount),
We make music, food, love.
We practice the protective,
Expressive, meditative arts.
We go for walks.

Nothing real can be lost.

TO BE REVOLUTIONARY

Who Am I
To be revolutionary?
Chinese and Jewish
Yoga pants meets Rock & Roll
Queer, crafty, prefers cold weather
Excitable about good ideas when high

Who Am I
To take revolution personally?
Like someone taking your baby
Without permission
So personal it splits you open
And your insides spill out
Everywhere

Though well-educated and well-fed
I've walked among the dead
Felt the shuddering clutches
Of systemic dysfunction
Peeled back the skin

Revolution wears many robes
Some folks take off for the front lines
For others, revolution sounds like jazz
And scissors cutting paper

For some, revolution feels like a strong headwind
For others, revolution simply blinks
Like the eye of a needle buried in haystacks

How do you breathe on stolen land?
How do you sleep on the backs of others?
The earth whispers its burdens
Forms tumors in the wombs of black women
The white men remove them
The cycle continues

Oppression looks like fashion
And the American dream
Revolution looks like an old woman
Dancing in the street

Oppression looks like manicured lawns
And ornamental trees
Revolution looks like rich soil
And heirloom seeds

Truth may set us free
But it can be terrifying
It holds up the mirror
Revolution is the broken glass

So I ask:
Who am I to be revolutionary?

But here's the better question:
Who am I not to be?

MOVING TO BRAMBLE MOUNTAIN

So, Dina and I relinquished our house in San Diego, and moved into the unknown. Dina took her kids in the minivan and road-tripped through California before flying off to Tulum, Mexico. I took my kids in the Corolla and drove north, into the mountains of Mendocino County, to a small organic family farm.

Bramble Mountain Farm is a 20-acre heirloom owned by a pair of good-humored lovebirds who built a charming strawbale house and birthed a son. Two other volunteers live on the farm full-time. Now that I'm here, our crew totals five adults and three children. We have several large gardens, an orchard of fruit trees, a tribe of chickens (and baby chicks!), a herd of goats (and baby goats!), a pack of dogs, an assortment of cats, a sweet little rabbit, and wildlife galore.

Exiting mainstream modern society and building a tiny house trailer on a rugged rural farm is A Major Adjustment. For one thing, there is no reliable internet or cellphone service; I drive twenty minutes in order to Facetime my parents. There are rattlesnakes, ticks, and mosquitos to contend with. Travel between the tiny house, outdoor kitchen, and outhouse involves multiple hilly hikes. The kids are covered in dirt, most of the time.

But we are fully immersed in the real work of regenerative farming and community building. My little ones get to enjoy nature-based education with the support of a Waldorf-inspired home school curriculum. I am learning about herbalism, permaculture, and animal husbandry. I pick wild arugula and stick it straight into my mouth, balancing the spice with a sweet cherry tomato, warm from the sun.

My belief (and now, my personal experience) is that deeply connecting with Mother Earth is the simplest way to recover our senses after living in a society that systematically separates us. Times of tremendous uncertainty, overwhelming fear, and great loss require enormous courage, strong faith, and profound awareness. The maps of the previous generation do not apply in this landscape. We must dust off our inner compasses, and listen to the stars.

We are
all
one of
a kind

A PUBLIC SERVICE ANNOUNCEMENT

DO NOT, under any circumstance,
Go back to normal.

The rat race has run its course.

No more forcing our way
Through time and space.

Dust off the cobwebs
Of outdated consciousness.

Put down the ghost stories,
Faded glory of warfare.

Why die to live?

Backed into the corner,
We must bravely step forward.

The road unfolds at your feet,

In your fingertips,
Before your eyes.

The human condition cries for help,
And we are the only hope.

So gather a few friends.
Show up and dig in.
Build bridges, find grooves.
Make waves, grow food.

If it's a question of finding yourself,
You're not a bit lost.
The cost of society
Might have been your identity,
But nothing that can be stolen
Is really worth having.

Redefine associations.
Reassign negotiations.

Think in terms of
Relevant relationship,
And general vitality.

Leap out into the playing field
Of sustainable regeneration.

Read the memos
Posted by The Mother.

Let your love affair with
The Universe be relentless.

Navigate milestones
In mindful overtones,
Connecting points of light
With a mind magnetized, electrified
By courage, and a brilliant vision.

The shift is the gift,
Opening in you.

What's here now
Is both more important
And more true
Than what we knew before.

It's perfectly safe to let your spirit soar.

That being said,
The new paradigm
Hangs by a thread.

What kicks up
In the wake
Of a shake-up like this
Will land on our heads.

We need to know
What our values hold.

We need to know
That we vote
With our focus, our time
And the things we buy.

This may be a world divided,
But at the end of the day
We lay side by side
In our graves,
Interdependent in all ways.

DO NOT, under any circumstance,
Cope with this crisis.

Coping is an oppositional
Force to change;
An adaptation that breeds
Blame, shame, haze, and fog.

Stay rooted in reality,
Not just rainbows.

Positivity that ignores pain
Is toxic.
Pain that ignores purpose
Is paralyzing.
It takes both sides.

So, then, rise from within.

Take your place
In the skin you've been given,
And move from your heart.

Together we're more
Than the sum of our parts.

THIS IS HOW WE DO IT

Amidst our unfolding stories
I notice a lightness emerging.
There is an unburdening here
that goes beyond catharsis.

The feeling in the room
is clear and courageous—
a rolling up of collective sleeves.
It is the beginning of a relationship.

We are revealing our wounds
to one another,
but rather than bursting an emotional dike
that sweeps us away in helpless despair,
and rather than attaching to
and amplifying our pain,
we let it dissolve:

> In our willingness to live together,
> even for a few moments,
> inside this shared reality.

In our willingness to hear each other,
without judgment or manipulation,
without invoking shallow affirmations.

We are all in our seats—
working, as Alice Walker says:
"Face-to-face, in words that have
expressive human eyes behind them."

WELCOME

Welcome to this
Strange and twisting
City

Concrete sprawl
Commercial distribution
Heavy traffic

Find your way
Through haze of
Artificial Stimulants
Smell of exhaust
High cost of living

Hungry Ghosts
In stylish clothes
Look shiny and smooth

WANTED:
Balance

WHEN GODS GO FOR WALKS

There was a cold grey pall to the sky as they walked along the shore. Heavy clouds threatened rain, and rumbling waves broke like thunder over a low tide. The smell of seaweed and saltwater mingled with fumes from a paper mill about a mile away. A few stubborn seagulls stalked the beach, searching for bits and pieces of rubbish, but most of the usual feathered crowd had found lodging elsewhere. It was an afternoon that seemed to resign itself to the end of the day.

"They aren't making it," she said with a furrowed brow. "We might as well pull the plug." Her bare feet moved carefully over thousands of tiny clams, the size of teeth, littered across the sand.

"That's not the point, Kalia." He continued, waxing metaphorical. "In a productive garden, each plant supports those around it by doing what it does naturally. With enough diversity, the garden manages itself, keeps itself in a system of checks and balances. You know, homeostasis."

"Yes, exactly. But we're looking at a junk yard."

"It's a mess right now, I know. But it's the tipping point. The shifting of the poles. And it's bringing up all the shit, specifically so that it can compost. Then, even the nastiest weeds get another chance."

She gave him a long look. Her eyes changed, from their usual vibrant blue to a blood-stain brown. He could see the pain moving behind them. It was a tired, lingering pain. An old pain. He met her gaze but said nothing. A flock of low-flying pelicans seemed to appear from nowhere, grazing the steel grey ocean in an uneven line.

"Each of us plays every part at different points, from the bees to the bugs to the blossoms to the bones. It all passes in due time," she said with an air of finality. "But the time has come, and they are due."

"And the day came when the risk it took to remain tight inside the bud was more painful than the risk it took to blossom," he said, quoting Anais Nin. "Let them be." A humid wind stirred, bringing a few drops of rain.

"But so few are blooming to their fullest expression, Jesse. It's just a restless urge to keep on living at all costs, because it's all they've got." She stopped to pick up a smooth, greenish-colored rock, and, brushing off the sand, handed to him.

Taking the rock with a small smile, he said, “It’s all they *think* they’ve got. But minds change. And our continued investment—our commitment, as gardeners—is to support their evolution.” He put the rock into his pocket. It would join the many others she had given him.

“Kalia,” he said gently, “how can you hold the blind accountable for what they don’t see?”

They walked in silence for a while. Then she said, “Every time I step foot onto that soil, my heart breaks."

He stopped and took her hand, pulling her around to face him. “But this is what we do. We tend the garden. We give it the opportunity of a lifetime. Then, when something shows a will to live, we water it.”

The rain began to fall in earnest.

PASSING ON

your eyes grew cloudy
and finally closed.
mouth hung open,
coated tongue,
feet mottled black.

I held your cold hand.

your raspy sips of breath
grew shallow
shrinking
a long pause—
I stopped breathing too—
and then,
one more vestigial inhalation
and a flash
of silver light
above your slackened jaw.

it was like watching a sunset.

dance, dear one
in the breeze between the leaves
of the cypress trees you loved.

visit me
in big blue dragonflies
in yellow butterflies
in birdsong.

FALLING INTO THE WILD

September begins.
I sit at a small table
along the rim of a redwood forest.
An extension cord
stretches over soft earth,
powering my computer,
the minifridge, and a lamp.
I've been camping for three months now.

Light filters
through a million different leaves.
Each tree has its own story,
yet they're all on the same page.
Mother nature at work.

People in the city work
hard to keep hold of their heads.
Endless methods for reconnecting brain to body.
How to breathe.
How to claim your power.
How to find your happiness.

Coaching is the new career.
If you leverage the internet correctly,
success is yours.

My full hat-rack.
Mother of Three Daughters.
Yoga Teacher. Writer. Editor.
Musician. Activist. Dancer.
All these Things to Do,
and People to Be.
How to merge your inner life
with your outer one
in a way that works.

And my soul, yearning to know:
Who am I, without the assumptions of the world?

HO'OPONOPONO

I'm sorry: for holding myself hostage
Forgive me: I simply forgot that I am worth being
Thank you: for timely reminders, gentle and firm
I love you, I love you, I love you

I'm sorry: for tampering with my own evidence
Forgive me: I thought I had something to prove
Thank you: for helping me drop the charges as filed
I love you, I love you, I love you

I'm sorry: for the senseless torture
Forgive me: I couldn't feel my own pain
Thank you: for holding tight until I could find it
I love you, I love you, I love you

I'm sorry: for criticism, doubt, and judgment
Forgive me: I did what I had been shown
Thank you: for rebuilding my infrastructure
I love you, I love you, I love you

I'm sorry: for delaying gratification
Forgive me: I was told it wasn't enough
Thank you: for every miraculous moment
I love you, I love you, I love you

GRACE

When she was little, she spoke to bees. She told them that her sister's doll had a green dress and hers had a red one, and she liked green better. She told them she saw her father in his underwear, and her mother said a swear word. She told them when she farted at school, how people laughed at her.

It was an intimate, comforting routine—and to her young mind, completely natural. Whenever she had something on her chest, she would begin to hear a buzzing in her head—and within a few moments, a bee would land on her shoulder. As she vented her various fears and frustrations, it would sit there, quietly absorbing her words. Once she had finished, the bee would fly off and leave her feeling relaxed, happy, and content to go about her childish business.

Eventually she started thinking about clothes, boys, and pop music. She forgot about bees. It wasn't until many years later, when the man she had loved was long gone and she was nose-to-the-grindstone, providing for two children and managing a household, that the buzz returned.

The phone call came at 3:17 in the afternoon. She was in the kitchen, trying to decide between mango chutney and pesto sauce. The voice on the other line was too calm.

Come as soon as you can, it said.

There weren't many cars on the interstate, but she felt like she was in traffic the entire way. She kept turning the radio on and off, up and down, station to station. Her fingers would alternately tap and squeeze the steering wheel. More than once, she realized she hadn't been breathing, and gasped.

Somehow she arrived at the same hospital where Sam was born, six years earlier. She remembered the doors—a strange shade of orangey red, not quite of this world. Now they were faded, chipped, and peeling. A nauseating stench, bleach mixed with anxiety, hung heavily in the hallway as she approached the nursing station for a room number.

Finally, Sam. Welts had risen all over his small body, and his eyes were swollen shut. Every inhalation seemed a struggle—his chest rose and fell in short, strangled spasms. The words "anaphylactic shock" bounced loosely through the air, refusing to land.

She wanted to pick Sam up and run away, but her feet had gone numb and cold along with the rest of her body. The doctor was a white smudge on a dark background, telling her in the calm voice that, for an anaphylactic reaction to occur, a person must have had prior exposure. Sam had gotten stung before, when he was about two years old, tottering through the yard in bare feet. He sat around whining for a bit, that was all, he was fine.

Minutes or days later she sat in an office staring at the floor.

The doctor had green shoelaces, the same color as Sam's eyes had been.

What followed was a blur; she remained numb and cold. Maybe it was anger. But whatever it was, she didn't shed a tear—not even at the funeral—and when extended family members had given their last hugs and gone home, and friends had stopped offering to cook meals, she began scraping herself together. It was slow going; at any turn she might bump into a sensation that reduced her to stone. She didn't know how long it was before she could read a whole story to her daughter at bedtime, or put away an entire load of laundry. Mostly she was afraid to move, lest the void within her grow bigger and swallow her whole.

At some point, however, she took up the habit of wandering in the woods behind her house. The morning light glinting off leaf-tops and the trilling of birds tore jagged pockets of stillness within her quailing mind, and it was from one of these openings that she heard a buzzing noise. It was faint at first, no more than a whispered hiss deep within her inner ear. But as she stopped to listen, it grew louder. Her entire body began to vibrate with it. Several moments later, a large bumblebee emerged from the foliage and settled onto her right shoulder.

For a split second she almost screamed. This was the very creature who instigated her grief—whose existence had erased Sam's. But confronted directly with its presence, something inside of her—the anger?—crumbled. Falling onto hands and knees, she cried so hard the force of it rocked her back and forth. She cried until every cell of her body emptied, until she was exhausted and weightless. The bee never moved.

By the time she got to her feet and stumbled home, the bee had departed. However, the once-fleeting pocket of stillness had grown and taken hold. There was a definite space within her, a calm that remained, even when she sat down to fold clothes, fresh from the dryer that night.

GROWING
IN

BODY OF WATER

I am a body of water
and my tears fall like rain
as I witness the pain of generations.
My arteries, like rivers
clotting, clogging, throbbing
in the aftermath of so much bad blood,
so much blood shed,
so many lives led to ruin
for the sake of a buck.

It's hard to feel stuck.
And it hurts to bleed so much.

But I am a body of water
and gradually, over time,
I will erode the barriers
that block my path.
I will soften rough edges
and find new openings,
whittle new ways of being,
for I am regenerative.

I am life and abundance and dancing.
I'm not here to be damned.
I don't want to be bottled and sold.
I want to run with the land.
Through seasons of flood
and seasons of drought,
going within and going without,
expanding and contracting with the moon,
carrying the tune of countless voices.

The choice is before us
and every drop counts.

Listen.
Bipolarity is not a disorder.
Duality is part of divine order:
It's what holds us together
in this vast ocean of consciousness,
the infinite deep,
where mysteries seep
through the pores of our skin.

I am devotion and community and hope.
I am up to my eyeballs with growth.

Eventually my body will evaporate,
but for now I just flow—
following the current
at the tip of my nose.

I am a body of water with a rising tide.
I want to lift as many ships as I can.
I want to stand and swirl and run and fall,
To wash over and through and between it all.

I am a body of water,
pooling at your feet.

It is very nice to meet you.

FULL CIRCLE

come one and all
on The Ride

admission is open
and free

there's the red horse
                    or giraffe, or whatever
and you want to get on it

the golden ring glimmers

The Ride being what it is
you fall off the horse
                    or giraffe, or whatever

whatever pulls you
back on board
is worth holding

At every step
of the way,
you are worth
every step.

MARRY ME

I have gathered myself here today,
(and every day, for decades)
to bear witness to the gift
opening at my feet—
The Present.

Asking the big question:
Will I marry me?

I commit to my YES.

I stand with myself
in sickness and health,
knowing that sickness
is an intelligent message from my body
and deserves to be treated with respect.

I celebrate my worth
when richer and poorer,
because really there's no such thing.
My value is inherent, innate,

and greater than all the money in the world.

I choose gratitude
for better or worse,
since judgment weaves spells of stagnation
any struggle is a perfect practice opportunity
to reframe my perception,
to sharpen my mindset,
and grow exponentially.

Quantum leaps are natural,
in nature.

I take me as is,
to love and to cherish,
having the time of my life—
until death do I
start again.

And so,
by the power of The Big Hand vested in me,
guiding and directing and protecting me,
leading me to this moment
and the sweetness of home,

I pronounce myself
Whole.

IN THE RAIN

In the rain,
I remember
quiet inside spaces.

The scent of release.

Sodden dreams,
warm drinks.

I remember
inky hands
after twisting newspapers
for the wood-burning stove,

the froth of wheels on the road,
and the wool-tickle
of scarf against my nose.

CLIMATE CHANGE

Last night I tripped hard and landed in 2051.

The panic was real and the devastation complete. Some say it was the quake, others point to government conspiracy. Most people just shook their heads and muttered something to the effect of "... this was coming." We didn't know where to look: at each other, or at our screens. Nobody could guess where help would come from, or how it would arrive, or when. The roads had been annihilated.

In the end it didn't matter what—or who—started it.

The water comes in and you find higher ground. But there are more people than peaks. Can you image a million desperate souls trying to climb Mount Soledad? If you happen to have a house up there, the easiest thing to do is fling open your doors and let them come in. Otherwise, they drag you out.

Some people witness indescribable horrors every day—but around here, we have soft feet. We have clean fingernails, new clothes, and cars. When something hap-

pens and we don't like it, we get into our cars and drive away.

But not today.

I saw a man shove a bottle into his crying baby's mouth so hard he snapped its little head back and killed it.

The water is still rising.

We were obsessed with the news. Commercial flights grounded; satellites commandeered for military use.

There were 44 left when the Navy ship finally found us. 31 men and 13 women. We never did see a Coast Guard. The Navy ship carried us away from the mountain top and for several days, nobody spoke. How do you break a silence when it is pregnant with your friends and family and pets? Some of us were already ghosts.

They gave us blankets and grilled cheese sandwiches. I threw up as soon as the bread touched my tongue.

The earth has shed its skin, again. That's what it does.

If only my own skin was thicker.

In my backpack I carried a tattered copy of "The Little Prince," one small white sandal, keys, and a dead flashlight. I had lost everything but my mind, but it was my mind that I wanted most to be rid of. I heard every bird, and every splash of water. I felt every nerve in my body scream.

We're fast, but nature is faster. Entire cities crumpled and smeared. You can keep going or you can give up, but you can't get out.

Another man sang softly to himself.

44 of us trying to hold it together.

The first night in the Navy ship was like trying to sleep a large family on a single cot. At first, people try to lie quietly. But you can't sleep and the more tired you become, the more likely you are to push the person next to you. Then one person's push is another's shove, and before you know it, the entire place is up in arms.

Eventually I found a corner and curled myself into a fist. My mother used to tell me God invented time so that everything didn't happen all at once—but now I realize that time really stands as a space holder, like zeroes after a decimal. It doesn't stop things from happening.

I woke up this morning and everything hurt.

In the absence
of fear,
there is Love.

GOING SOULAR

You,
The Human Being,
Are a little working model of the universe—
A microcosm of the macrocosm.

And this
Is a matter of economics.

Reduce your dependence
On non-renewable energy.
Develop self-sustainability.

Soular Power is
        Non-toxic.
        Organic.
        Fair Trade.

Plus,
It is already
Hard-wired
Into your system.

RECIPROCAL RELATIONS

he doesn't need her to lean on him,
in order to feel his own strength.

and she doesn't need to lean,
in order to feel his support.

OLIVE

Near Chesapeake Hall grows a stand of olive trees.
They are bisected by the road that cuts through
town so that some grow in a grassy median,
others along the sidewalk.

People, in cars or on foot,
pass back and forth.
They peer straight ahead
or into cellular phones
as they scuttle along.
They are unaware of the olive trees.
But the trees are very aware of the people.

The ripe olives fall,
creating a lumpy groundcover
that thousands of shoe-bottoms
will track into oblivion.

Any one of these olives
could have been sitting atop a sumptuous salad
or basking in a martini.

Any one of them
might have been pressed into oil
by a loving hand.

Along the sidewalk,
one olive tree is much smaller—
easily half the size of the others.

While its kin sprouted and began to grow,
impatient for the glories
of great heights and bright sunlight—
this tree sat in the soil and contemplated the dirt.

For seven summers it deferred,
listening to the rumblings of the earth.
It nearly stayed there, dormant,
hushed to sleep by the lullaby.
But something in the song
it heard finally compelled it to emerge.

Now, as people hurry past,
the little tree observes them.
It hears their hopes, fears, worries, and desires.
It wants to share something of the song.
It drops its olives in rhythm.

ADDICTED

Ah, there—
Here,
I was stuck.
So much resistance
Built up over this area.
And this one.
And that one,
Too.

Here is where
My life force
Pools,
Nudging me desperately
To dislodge it,
Because it wants to flow.

The old fix
Was to dislodge myself instead.
Move my head out of the way
With chemicals, ingestibles,
So I could forget

My discomfort
For a moment.
Convert it to pleasure,
Right on the spot.

Hit the spot, too,
Until it didn't.

Until the spot itself was sore.
Until the healing I was desperate for
Was from my own self-destruction.

Because self-destruction doesn't flow.
It spirals and dances and pushes and pulls.
But it doesn't flow.

My life force wants to flow—
Demands, requires, insists upon flow.
My life force has a dance all its own.
My life force has a song, a story, a purpose, a goal,
A gift, in fact, that only flow opens.

Flow comes in all forms.

Breath:
Readily available.
Your basic flow.

Movement:
Occupying the body

In conscious space and time.

Creativity:
Making something up,
So you can feel it dribble down
From your fingers,
Or your chin.

Connection:
Really being with another living thing.
(It's an exponential life force multiplier.)

And Love:
Anywhere love lives,
Life flows.

Now I know,
These sticky spots,
These irksome, tedious, shadowy smudges
Are built-in nudges—
Pestering me toward my potential,
Poking me to greater things,
Prodding me into the light,
Where I can see what I'm doing.

THOU
ART.

THE CALLING

This is a calling
To bare arms
Roll up your sleeves and dig in
The task at hand is no cake-walk
But you get the whole pie

This is a calling
To put down your load
Pick up your cross
You are your own salvation

This is a calling
To the inner ear
Collect
Feel the beat of your drum

This is a calling
To wake up
Open your mind's eye
Stop holding yourself remote
And get with the program

This is role call
Who is present?

THE PURPLE PICKLE

It was the process, not the product, that satisfied my young impulse. Pulling paper from the printer, gripping the hole-studded strips along the sides, bending them along the perforated lines, and then carefully ripping them off. Admiring the blank sheet that remained, so pristine and fresh. Deciding how many pages to prepare. Making a stack of suitable thickness and then folding it in half. Stapling the newly-formed spine, three times, close to the edge, evenly spaced.

At seven years old, The Purple Pickle was one of my favorite rituals. I made countless editions of this book, and never finished one. I revered concept and implementation: having generated the book itself, I'd design an engaging cover. Then, still salivating with imaginative juices, I would begin the content: laying out text and imagery, introducing the main character, launching a plot. Three, maybe four good pages tops. After that, writing and illustration became a chore, and I abandoned the project in search of new entertainment.

Perhaps, I put the book down with the intention to return someday, pick up where I'd left off. When that day came, I would lovingly caress its stapled spine, allow my eyes to linger on the title, taking in each letter, remembering their curves. Sensing anticipation build within me: the impetus to create. Feeling it pulse through my veins, heating my blood, ready to burst the instant my pencil? pen? touched the page. Flipping with tingling fingers through the previous pages, so strong, so complete, so ready to move forward...then finding the one that started to slip—an illustration with no color, a half-finished sentence. In that moment, I would enter with my pencil? pen? and begin again. I would tell the story. I would deliver the message. I would row the boat ashore.

LEST YOU LOSE COUNT

For those with the leisure
Of worrying about which party to attend,
what to wear, or how to eat less food—

For those who run out of space
To store pictures on their phones—

For those so constantly surrounded
By great ideas that they become overwhelmed—

For those blessed
With children who disappoint with
their attitudes, grades, or choice of music—

For those healthy enough
To take their bodies for granted—

For those who are deeply loved, respected,
cared for, and protected
By imperfect people—

It helps to stop,
If only once in the day,
And give thanks.

All the world has problems.
But of all the problems in the world,
These are a privilege.

Wake up one
day at a
time.

LIGHT THE FIRE

Fire, fire
Alchemical flame
Burning through shame
So we can be clear
Here and now

It's funny how
Fire speaks
In tongues
Licking some
Lashing some
Secret language of change
The metamorphosis game
Here you see me
Here you don't
Here I fly
But here I choke
The smoke gets thick in mirrors

Here, take a seat by the fire

Listen to the tongue of transformation
Let it smack your inner ear
Release the fear of losing fingers
When you reach for what you want and need

In the flicker of light
The dancing of shadows
We all watch the show
Though the human experience
Must be felt for itself
Wouldn't you know
The fear is the fire
The pain makes us whole

Listen to the space around the fire
It's perfectly still
And watch what you say
Because only words kill
The smoke is just a mirror

Here, take a seat in the fire

It tells us our story
And in glory, for glory
We burn

When it's your turn
Step light to the flame
When the tongue calls your name
Say "Aw, Men"

And then
Let the fire burn you alive
Burn you to life
Keep you warm, glowing, cozy inside
Give you new vision
Answer your prayers
Open your heart
And raise your awareness
Let the fire burn

And until it's your turn
Keep chopping the wood
Stoking the embers
Remember
What goes up in flames
Comes down in rain

FLIGHT PATH

Just like that,
        She jumped.
And just like that,
        She flew.

Of course, in the moment before she flew,
She truly felt she was falling.
Dying, even.
Drowning in liminal space.

Nothing to hold.
No worn trail.
Not even a groove.
(At least, not one proven safe.)

New muscle memory in the making—
Hinted at, only,
In the depths of some
Divinely-incepted intuitive cranny.

Ultimately,
It was the courage to dive
Deep beneath
That rose her to
New heights.

it's a
pleasure
being human
with you

MAKE PEACE

Just keep in mind,
The Earth whispered,
Between frost-tipped blades of grass:
Everything is an expression of Life—
Even death,
Even dying,
Even disease.

We must stop fearing these things.
Otherwise, we cannot
Express the Life
Within us,
That is, who we are
At the essential core of our beings.

Make peace
With the moment at hand—
For it will hold you
And guide you
And anchor you.

Accept what is already done.
Focus on what you are doing—
Which is a lot.
Which is everything.

Who are you with,
What are you working toward,
And what is it for?

You are a Product of Nature,
Growing riper and
Wilder by the year.
Forgetting spells cast
By masses
Who confused wealth with money
And power with control.

But look here:
Across all of history,
Evidence shows
That it only takes focused engagement
From 3% of a population
To make major change.
That, in fact, if 3% of the population engages
Then change is inevitable, guaranteed.

So pick your team,
Play your part.
Plant the seed of courage deep.
No tyranny can keep you from growing,

From showing up strong
In what you belong to,
Which is Life itself—
Directly felt in the fire, water,
Earth, air, and spirit.

You are a servant of the sacred ways—
Of clear, focused engagement.
And if you pass away today
Or decades from now,
Whether you go out healthy and kicking
Or flat on your back,
Your life is a victory
For you have recovered
The core of your being.

PATIENCE

Deep swirling waters
Demand strong clear strokes
Kicking in rhythm
Breathing with purpose

I'm equipped for this journey
Even when I don't know what's coming
Or when the gut-wrenching turmoil will settle
Back into stillness

EMERGENT ACQUISITIONS

The first time I merged creative writing
with the task of caring for children,
I got pulled over by the cops.
Pushing a stroller through suburbia,
stopping periodically to jot in my journal,
neighbors suspected me of casing garages.
Somebody reported,
a squad car pulled up,
I showed the officer I was taking notes
on the nature of the human experience,
and he pulled away.

I was left with the impression
of not being trusted or accepted
By my community as a mother.
Because I act, look, or sound different.
Because I like cannabis or I have tattoos.
And it triggered core wounds.
As an adolescent I heard the same tune.
As an infant, I cried alone in my room.

Such damage to my root sprouted decades
of dedicated self-destruction; in fact
the me you see now is still under reconstruction.

I've learned, however, to remove my hard-hat.
To step onto the scene in bare feet, heart open.
I've learned to bear down when I choke up,
To breathe myself home.
It's hard sometimes.
I do it anyway.

I've learned to get naked in front of other women
not because I want to touch their beautiful bodies,
but because I want to honor the beauty in my own.

Becoming a mother has taught me
to look deeper into my body for its beauty.

To look past the nicks and scratches and sags
on the surface.
To feel the power of surrender,
the strength of flexibility,
and the wisdom of compassion.
To know the process of letting go,
moving slow, honoring flow.
To listen with my inner ear.
To see with my 3rd eye.
To navigate with the tip of my crown.

I'm learning to ground.
To open the moment
as the gift that it is,
and in this SPACE,
to receive the richly rewarding experience
of expanded conscious capacity
for love, and laughter, and pain, and fear.
To be HERE with, for, and through it all.

But I sometimes question my intention,
interrogate myself senseless, relentless.
Sometimes I sort of crumple inside,
maybe die a few times, it's hard to describe.
Sometimes I have to take a time out just to tune in,
find a comfortable position again.
The things we carry get heavy.

But many hands make light work.
Let's pick up our tools and take out our pens,
put down our goggles and focus our lens.
Let's put our light to work.
Illuminate the path ahead.
This journey of humanity,
This having of a Self.
At the end of the day I don't know what else to do
besides whip out my journal and jot a few:
notes, chords, bar-lifter-uppers,
strategies, reminders, memos, instructions,
formulas, acronyms, symbols, equations,
sketches and maps to internal destinations.

Capturing that which is wild, raw, and real
so it can help set me free,
help me to feel.

I love being here in this body with you,
And I hope when you read this,
you love yourself too.

WHAT YOU
GET
IS WHAT YOU
SEE

LAST WORDS FIRST

We talk of transformation:
Making our way from one form to the next.

We attach to the new form:
Look how free I am now!

We fly for a while,
Then we hit a glass window.

The window is tangible or intangible,
Visible or invisible.
It crashes into our comfort zones and shatters
Our models for reality.
It's unnerving, a shock to the system.
We may find ourselves in depression.

What is real?
Who am I?
What's the point?
We feel a deep sense of loss.

I want to speak to this moment:
The dark night of the awakened soul.

Here's all I know, so far.
Depression is a sacred messenger
Of Unmet Needs.
It lets us know that we're ready to stop
What we are "doing" and grieve.

When our attachments, desires and dreams
Regarding people, places and things
Stop bringing us happiness or peace
The mind then judges our experience as "wrong."
There is nothing wrong.

Patterns that worked in old paradigms
Fall apart to make way for new growth.
As they do,
We seem to lose ourselves.
We may think of death.
Quite right.
An aspect of Self is passing on.
Grieve. Sit. Rest. Listen. Release.

Transformation is not a one-time thing.
It's not an end goal.
It's a continual unfolding,
A shedding of layers and skins.

When the time comes,
(And it will, again and again),
Reach out.
Speak up.
Ask for support.
Be seen.
We deserve to be loved, witnessed, and held
In all phases of our life cycle.

WORKING FORWARD

The thoughts, words, and actions
we choose for ourselves
have a significant impact
on the experience of our lives.

We might downplay the potency
of our thoughts,
but they inform our perception.

We might downplay the potency
of our words,
but they shape our connections.

We might downplay the potency
of our actions,
but they determine our outcomes.

May we all have the courage
to feel life as it comes.

CATCH YOUR BREATH

THE BEATEN PATH

As the beaten path
Falls behind in the distance,
The sound of a million men,
Marching like ants,
Fades from existence.

There is no end
To the beginning in sight.

PROCLAMATION

I may not be perfect,
But I am worthy
Of forgiveness, success, and grace.

I am worthy of my sacred fire,
And my sacred rage.

I choose to behave in constructive ways
With people who are committed
To reciprocity
And right relations.

I own my story and my stance.
I dance with the moment at hand.

I am a steward of life,
And a maker of love.

I'm here for the work,
And there's work to be done.

One step,
One choice,
One breath at a time.

One reason,
One resource,
One rhythm,
One rhyme.

SHIT HAPPENS

We need the shit.
It's the fertilizer.
Bring it up for air
so it can compost properly
and fuel our growth.

It's an asset,
and totally transformative.

So when shit hits the fan,
don't take it personally.
It's just par for the course
on the Orgone trail.

The plot thickens when
we've been taught to bury our shit,
or hold it in, or throw it, or sit in it,
or pretend it isn't ours.
But in fact it charges us.
It's what we tend to go on.

Alleviate the constipation of a nation.
The grass is greener on the other side
of the divide between heart and mind,
where the soul smiles in satisfaction
because it's gaining circulation, clearing space,
developing capacity, and clarifying intention.

Simply reminding us that this too shall pass.

If we think our shit is wrong
then we'll never get it right.
We need to keep sight of the fact
that it's all one tract,
it's all one system—
And if we simply relax
around the contraction,
align with the divine timing of action,
we'll get out of this shit-hole alive
and thrive, like Mother Nature intended.

WILLING
TO WORK
FORWARD

Gina Tang is based in San Diego, California. She lives in a tiny home office on a farm, and travels widely for purposes of cross-pollination.

The Regenerative Writing Institute is an independent publishing agency dedicated to supporting voices for hope, change, and resilience. We welcome manuscripts from authors, artists, and activists on a mission to share their message.

www.regenwriting.com

www.ingramcontent.com/pod-product-compliance
Ingram Content Group UK Ltd.
Pitfield, Milton Keynes, MK11 3LW, UK
UKHW020415250726
13967UKWH00007B/2657

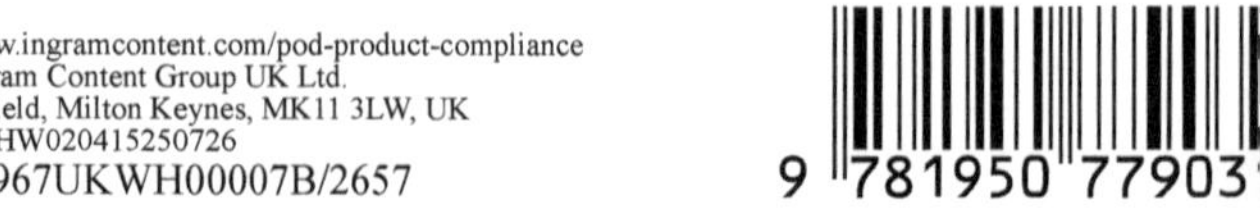

9 781950 77903